H ing
G ards

Annelies Karduks

FORTE PUBLISHERS

© 2005 Forte Uitgevers, Utrecht
© 2005 for the translation by the publisher
Original title:
Harmonicakaarten nieuwe stijl

All rights reserved.
No part of this publication may be copied, stored in an electronic file or made public, in any form or in any way whatsoever, either electronically, mechanically, by photocopying or any other form of recording, without the publisher's prior written permission.

ISBN 90 5877 634 4

This is a publication from
Forte Publishers BV
P.O. Box 1394
3500 BJ Utrecht
The Netherlands

For more information about the creative books available from Forte Publishers:
www.forteuitgevers.nl

Final editing: Gina Kors-Lambers, Steenwijk, the Netherlands
Photography and digital image editing: Fotografie Gerhard Witteveen, Apeldoorn, the Netherlands
Cover and inner design: BADE creatieve communicatie, Baarn, the Netherlands
Translation: Michael Ford, TextCase, Hilversum, the Netherlands

Contents

Preface	3
Techniques	4
Materials	5
Step-by-step	6
Name cards	7
White flowers	10
Flowers	12
Harmonica	14
Roses	18
Butterflies	20
Christmas layer cards	22
Christmas	26
Cards on pages 1 and 3	30
Patterns	31

Preface

The third series of harmonica templates and rulers deserves a third book to show all the possibilities they offer. To show you that all the templates and rulers can be used together, I have used the templates from the second series together with the rulers from the third series.

The different methods of decorating the cards which the templates offer, in combination with lace stickers, scrapbook paper, etc. guarantee some very special cards.

See page 32 if you wish to remain informed of what I have in store for you in the future.

I wish you lots of fun with these harmonica cards.

Annelies Karduks

Thanks to William, Robine and Larissa, for all your enthusiasm!

Techniques

Carefully read the instructions given below and look at the *Step-by-step* photographs before you start.

Guide lines on the templates
- The templates are 14.85 cm high and they can be used to cut the cards to the correct size.
- There is a line on the templates which indicates the middle.
- The templates have two lines which are 10.5 cm apart. If you make a card which is 10.5 cm high, then you must keep the bottom line level with the bottom of the card and the top line level with the top of the card.
- There are two arrows on the second and third series of templates (no. 3705 to 3712) which are 6 cm apart.

Using the harmonica rulers
Choose the card you wish to make. Read the instructions and cut the card to the correct size. The instructions also tell you which harmonica ruler to use. The harmonica rulers are drawn on the packaging of the templates. Use the ruler to draw lines at the top and bottom of the card. On the harmonica ruler, it is indicated which lines to use to cut shapes and which lines to use to make uninterrupted score lines. Score the uninterrupted score lines first to avoid making any mistakes (see photograph 1).

Cutting a harmonica card
Look on the ruler for a < -sign or a > -sign. The < -sign indicates that the shape faces to the left and the > -sign indicates that the shape faces to the right. Use template tape to stick the harmonica template level with the lines farthest to the left. Cut the shape(s) and score the straight lines using the template or a ruler (see photograph 2). Repeat this for the next lines with a < -sign or a > -sign. It is important not to cut through the uninterrupted score lines.
To avoid doing so, use the smaller cutting shape (see photograph 3).

Folding the card
Fold the uninterrupted score lines first and then the score lines interrupted by shapes. On the ruler, you will see whether you must make a valley fold or a mountain fold (see photograph 4). When you have finished, rub the lines out. All the harmonica cards, except for the swing cards, fit into a normal envelope. Fold the cards double along the uninterrupted score lines to make them fit into an envelope.

Decorating the card
The harmonica templates can be used in different ways to decorate the cards.

Embossing
Cut the shapes out as explained in the instructions. Stick the template to a light box. Use template tape to stick the shape on the template with the good side facing downwards and copy the illuminated shapes

using the embossing stylus. If you want, you can use Pergasoft to make the embossing easier.

Cutting
Hold a sharp knife vertically when cutting the lines in the template. Remove the template and cut through every other middle piece.

Cutting half-shapes
Place the template level with the edge of the card so that only the shape is on the card and then cut out the half-shape.

Cutting shapes
Place the template on a piece of card. Use a pencil to draw along the straight lines of the template and mark the middle point. Cut half of the shape. Rotate the template, place it level with the lines and the middle point and cut out the other half.

Materials

- *Card and paper:*
  cArt-us (CA), Canson Mi-Teintes (C) and Papicolor (P) (the colour number is stated with the instructions of every card)
- *Harmonica templates*
- *Scoring pen*
- *Cutting ruler with a metal edge*
- *Cutting mat*
- *Hobby knife*
- *Template tape*
- *3D cutting sheets*
- *Tweezer scissors*
- *Photo glue*
- *3D foam tape/blocks of 3D foam tape and/ or silicon glue*
- *Light box*
- *Embossing stylus*
- *Pergasoft*
- *Eyelet tool*
- *Eyelet hammer*
- *Pencil*
- *Rubber*
- *Non-permanent Pritt*
- *Xyron 150*
- *Xyron 250*
- *Zip'eMate*

Step-by-step

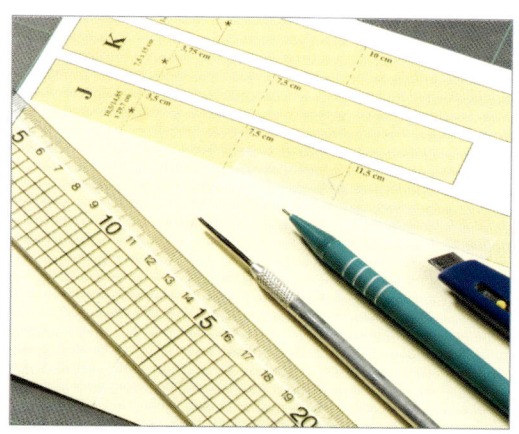

1. Draw lines using the harmonica ruler and score the uninterrupted score lines.

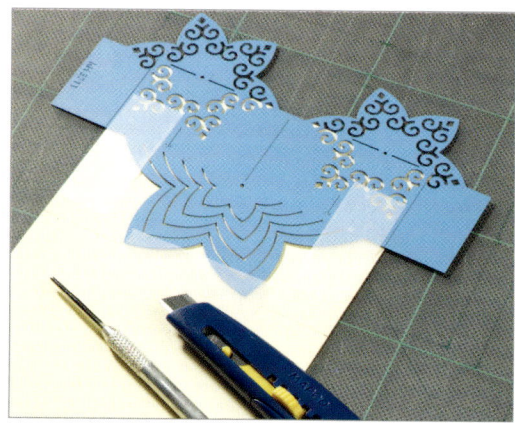

2. Stick the harmonica template level with the lines farthest to the left and cut the shape.

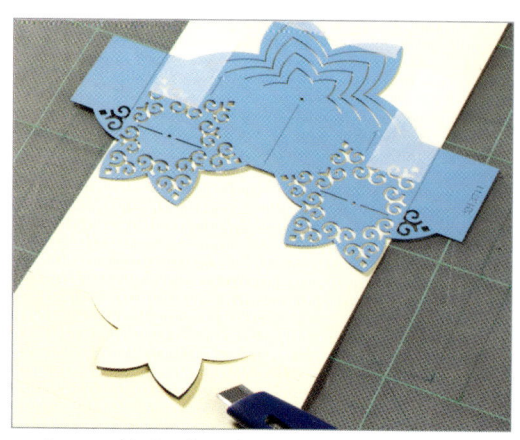

3. Repeat this for the other lines.

4. Fold the card and rub the lines out.

Name cards

Thea & Hans

What you need
- *cArt-us card: pink 481 (P34)*
- *Bazzill card: pomegranate 227 (P43)*
- *Harmonica templates: no. 10 flower 2 and no. 12 flower 4, Ruler K*
- *Sirius frame sheet: white and pink flowers (SHSV223)*
- *Zip'eMate, Sizzlits alphabet: playground*
- *Hole punch: medium*
- *Mini adhesive stones: pink*

Instructions

1. Cut the card to size (7.5 x 15 cm). Cut, score and fold the harmonica card. Mark the middle of the first two lines and place one of the twin shapes level with this mark.

2. Cut a 6 cm flower shape for Thea and a 4.5 cm flower shape for Hans out of card. Cut a 4.5 cm flower shape for Thea and a 3 cm flower shape for Hans out of the cutting sheet. Cut a pomegranate strip (1 x 7.5 cm)

3. Punch the letters and put them through the Xyron sticker maker. Put a piece of cutting sheet and a piece of pomegranate card through the Xyron sticker maker. Punch the dots.

4. Stick everything on the card. Use adhesive stones to decorate the card.

W & A

What you need
- Bazzill card:
  stonewash 744 (P42) and admiral 783 (P41)
- Harmonica templates:
  no. 5 labels and no. 7 triangles
- Ruler K
- Sirius frame sheet:
  pink and purple flowers (SHSV220)
- Zip'eMate
- Wafer dies Alphabet Jellybean: capitals 5/8"
- Easy punch daisy: yellow
- Easy punch daisy: green
- Eyelets: monochromatic blue
- Mini adhesive stones: pink

Instructions

1. Cut the card to size (7.5 x 15 cm). Cut, score and fold the harmonica card. Mark the middle of the first two lines and place one of the twin shapes level with this mark.

2. Cut a 6 cm high label and a 5 cm high triangle out of card. Cut a 5 cm high label and a 4 cm high triangle out of the cutting sheet. Cut strips and punch daisies for decoration.

3. Punch the letters and put them through the Xyron sticker maker.

4. Stick everything on the card and add some eyelets. Use adhesive stones to decorate the card.

Jesse & Diana

What you need
- *Bazzill card:*
  stonewash 744 (P42) and admiral 783 (P41)
- *Harmonica templates:*
  no. 9 flower 1 and no. 11 flower 3
- *Ruler K*
- *Sirius frame sheet:*
  pink and purple flowers (SHSV220)
- *Zip'eMate*
- *Sizzlits mat*
- *Sizzlits alphabet script*
- *Mini adhesive stones: light blue*

Instructions
1. Cut the card to size (7.5 x 15 cm). Cut, score and fold the harmonica card. Mark the middle of the first two lines and place one of the twin shapes level with this mark.

2. Cut a 6 cm flower shape out of admiral card and a 4.5 cm flower shape out of the frame sheet.

3. Punch the letters and put them through the Xyron sticker maker.

4. Stick everything on the card. Use adhesive stones to decorate the card.

White flowers

Roses

What you need
- Doublemates card: groovy grape
- Mi-Teintes card: white 335 (P30)
- Harmonica template: no. 6 flowers
- Ruler L
- Sticker sheet: lilac flower lace borders
- Stamp: rose
- Stamp-pad ink: heliotrope, lime and green
- Transparent embossing powder
- Heat gun

Instructions

1. Cut the card to size (14.8 x 29.7 cm). Cut, score and fold the harmonica card. Use the side with the two shapes, one under the other.

2. Stick two strips (1 x 14.8 cm) on the card. Use stickers to decorate the card.

3. Stamp the roses. Sprinkle embossing powder on them and cut them out. Use green stamp-pad ink to decorate the flowers.

4. Stick the flowers on the card and make them 3D.

Flowers

What you need
- *Doublemates card: groovy grape*
- *Mi-Teintes card: white 335 (P30)*
- *Harmonica template: no. 12 flowers 4*
- *Ruler L*
- *Decorative sticker: lilac lace pattern no. 2*
- *Stamp: flower background*
- *Stamp-pad ink: heliotrope*
- *Transparent embossing powder*
- *Heat gun*

Instructions

1. Cut the card to size (14.8 x 29.7 cm). Cut, score and fold the harmonica card. Use the side with the two shapes, one under the other.

2. Stick two strips (1 x 14.8 cm) on the card. Use stickers to decorate the card.

3. Stamp the largest flowers. Sprinkle embossing powder on them and cut them out leaving a small border. Use circle stickers to decorate the flowers.

4. Use foam tape or silicon glue to stick the flowers on the card.

Flowers

Anemones

What you need
- cArt-us card: white 210 (P30)
- Bazzill card: petunia 140 and Hillary 511
- Harmonica template: no. 9 flower 1
- Ruler I
- Marjoleine cutting sheet: pink anemones
- Decorative paper: green/pink stripes
- Decorative stickers: hearts

Instructions

1. Cut the card to size (14.85 x 21 cm). Cut, score and fold the harmonica card. Cut the smallest shape at the first > -sign, cut the 6 cm shape (indicated by arrows) at the second > -sign and cut the outer shape at the third > -sign.

2. Stick 1.5 cm wide pink strips on the card and decorate them with 1 cm wide strips of decorative paper.

3. Cut the shapes and stick them on the card. Use sticker hearts to decorate the shapes.

4. Use foam tape or silicon glue to stick the anemones on the card.

12

Roses

Instructions

1. Cut the card to size (14.85 x 21 cm). Cut, score and fold the harmonica card. Cut the smallest shape at the first > -sign, cut the 6 cm shape (indicated by arrows) at the second > -sign and cut the outer shape at the third > -sign.

2. Stick 1.5 cm wide green strips on the card and decorate them with 1 cm wide strips of decorative paper.

3. Cut the shapes and stick them on the card. Use circle stickers to decorate the shapes.

4. Use foam tape or silicon glue to stick the roses on the card.

What you need
- cArt-us card:
  white 210 (P30) and golden yellow 247 (P10)
- Bazzill card: ivy 589
- Harmonica template: no. 11 flower 3
- Ruler I
- Marjoleine cutting sheet: yellow roses
- Decorative paper: brown stripes
- Decorative stickers: circles

Harmonica

Marigolds

What you need
- *cArt-us card: golden yellow 247 (P10) and dark blue 417 (P41)*
- *Harmonica template: no. 5 labels, Ruler J*
- *Brodery template no. 7, Pattern A*
- *Perforating tools (fine and extra fine) and pricking mat*
- *Sulky thread (gold 7007) and pearl needles*
- *Round eyelets: monochromatic yellow*
- *Shake it images cutting sheet: yellow flowers IT427*
- *Zip'eMate*
- *Wafer dies Alphabet Jellybean: capitals 5/8"*

Instructions
1. Cut the card to size (10.5 x 29.7 cm). Cut, score and fold the harmonica card using the cutting lines with the arrows.

2. Cut three dark blue strips (two of 1.5 x 10.5 cm and one of 4 x 10.5 cm) and mark the middle of the long sides. Place the middle of one of the patterns on the template level with the middle of the strip and prick the pattern. Embroider the second pattern from the right. Stick the strips on the card.

3. Use pattern A to cut four labels. Use eyelets to attach them to the card. Punch the letters and prick the holes. Put them through the Xyron sticker maker and stick them on the card. Use foam tape or silicon glue to stick the flowers on the card.

Hibiscus

Instructions

1. Cut the card to size (10.5 x 29.7 cm). Cut, score and fold the harmonica card using the cutting lines with the arrows.

2. Put a piece of dark blue card and a piece of yellow card through the Xyron sticker maker. Cut four dark blue strips (1.5 x 10.5 cm) and four yellow strips (0.5 x 10.5 cm). Stick all the strips on the card.

3. Cut four flower shapes. Wind embroidery thread around them and stick them on the card. Use foam tape or silicon glue to stick the flowers on the card.

What you need
- cArt-us card: golden yellow 247 (P10) and dark blue 417 (P41)
- Harmonica template: no. 10 flower 2
- Ruler J
- Sulky thread: gold 7007
- Shake it images cutting sheet: yellow flowers IT427

Daisies

Instructions

1. Cut the card to size (10.5 x 29.7 cm). Cut, score and fold the harmonica card using the cutting lines with the arrows.

2. Put a piece of dark green card and a piece of scrapbook paper through the Xyron sticker maker. Cut eight strips of scrapbook paper (four of 1.5 x 10.5 cm and four of 1 x 10.5 cm). Score the narrow strips. Cut four dark green strips (1 x 10.5 cm). Stick everything on the card.

3. Cut and emboss four triangles and stick them on the card. Use foam tape or silicon glue to stick the flowers on the card. Add the Brads.

What you need
- cArt-us card: dark green 309 (P18) and spring green 305 (P08)
- Harmonica template: no. 7 triangles
- Ruler J
- Scrap pad: Clarity
- Shake it images cutting sheet: white flowers IT429
- Flower Brads: monochromatic yellow

Chrysanthemums

Instructions

1. Cut the card to size (10.5 x 29.7 cm). Cut, score and fold the harmonica card using the cutting lines with the arrows.

2. Put a piece of dark green card and a piece of scrapbook paper through the Xyron sticker maker. Cut four strips of scrapbook paper (0.5 x 10.5 cm). Punch two sets of twelve squares. Stick everything on the card.

3. Cut and emboss four flower shapes and stick them on the card. Use foam tape or silicon glue to stick the flowers on the card. Use adhesive stones to decorate the card.

What you need
- cArt-us card: dark green 309 (P18) and spring green 305 (P08)
- Harmonica template: no. 12 flower 4
- Ruler J
- Scrap pad: Clarity
- Easy punches: orange and green square
- Shake it images cutting sheet: white flowers IT429
- Mini adhesive stones: warm yellow

Roses

Rose

What you need
- Doublemates card: spring green
- Harmonica template: no. 11 flower 3
- Ruler L
- Marij Rahder cutting sheet: rose V2566

Instructions

1. Cut the card to size (14.8 x 29.7 cm). Cut, score and fold the harmonica card using the side with the single shape. Cut the decorations by cutting all the cutting lines of the single shape. Cut out every other piece of decoration. Put the cut out pieces through the Xyron sticker maker.

2. Cut a 9 cm flower shape.

3. Cut the strips out of the cutting sheet.

4. Stick all the parts on the card. Stick a picture of a rose on the card and make it 3D.

Rosebud

What you need
- Doublemates card: spring green
- Harmonica template: no. 10 flower 2
- Ruler L
- Marij Rahder cutting sheet: rose V2566

Instructions

1. Cut the card to size (14.8 x 29.7 cm). Cut, score and fold the harmonica card using the side with the single shape. Cut the decorations by cutting all the cutting lines of the single shape. Cut out every other piece of decoration. Put the cut out pieces through the Xyron sticker maker.

2. Cut a 7.5 cm flower shape.

3. Cut the corner pieces out of the cutting sheet.

4. Stick all the parts on the card. Stick a picture of a rose on the card and make it 3D.

Butterflies

Orange tip

What you need
- cArt-us card: dark blue 417 (P41), ochre 575 (P26) and natural 211 (P29)
- Harmonica template: no. 11 flower 3
- Ruler J
- Mini ornament line stickers: gold no. 2
- Wire & Wire
- Shake it images cutting sheet: purple flowers IT430

Instructions

1. Cut the card to size (10.5 x 29.7 cm). Cut, score and fold the harmonica card using the cutting lines with the arrows.

2. Cut five ochre strips (two of 2.2 x 10.5 cm, two of 2.5 x 10.5 cm and one of 5 x 10.5 cm). Score the narrow strips. Stick all the strips on the card and decorate them with line stickers.

3. Cut and emboss four flower shapes and stick them on the card. Use Wire & Wire to make the antennae. Use foam tape or silicon glue to stick the butterflies on the card.

Meadow brown

Instructions

1. Cut the card to size (10.5 x 29.7 cm). Cut, score and fold the harmonica card using the cutting lines with the arrows.

2. Cut five ochre strips (two of 2.2 x 10.5 cm, two of 3.2 x 12 cm and one of 6 x 12 cm). Score the narrow strips and punch the other strips. Stick the strips on the card and cut them so that they are level with the edge of the card. Decorate them with line stickers.

3. Cut and emboss four flower shapes and stick them on the card. Use foam tape or silicon glue to stick the butterflies on the card.

What you need
- cArt-us card: dark blue 417 (P41) and natural 211 (P29)
- cArt-us paper: ochre 575 (P26)
- Harmonica template: no. 9 flower 1
- Ruler J
- Mini ornament line stickers: gold no. 2
- Border emboss punch: flowers
- Shake it images cutting sheet: yellow flowers IT427

Christmas layer cards

Christmas decorations

What you need
- cArt-us card: white 210 (P30)
- Bazzill card: pansy 640
- Harmonica template: no. 8 stars
- Ruler I
- Pattern B
- Marjoleine cutting sheet: purple Christmas
- Decorative border stickers: silver wyber
- Round Brads: silver

Instructions

1. Cut the card to size (14.85 x 21 cm). Cut, score and fold the harmonica card. Cut the smallest shape at the first > -sign, cut the 6 cm shape (indicated by arrows) at the second > -sign and cut the outer shape at the third > -sign.

2. Stick 1.5 cm wide pansy strips on the card and decorate them with stickers.

3. Use pattern B to cut the half-shapes and stick them to the back of the card.

4. Use foam tape or silicon glue to stick the Christmas decorations on the card. Add the Brads.

22

Christmas bells

Instructions

1. Cut the card to size (14.85 x 21 cm). Cut, score and fold the harmonica card. Cut the smallest shape at the first > -sign, cut the 6 cm shape (indicated by arrows) at the second > -sign and cut the outer shape at the third > -sign.

2. Stick 1.5 cm wide pansy strips on the card and decorate them with stickers.

3. Use pattern C to cut the half-shapes and stick them to the back of the card.

4. Use foam tape or silicon glue to stick the Christmas bells on the card.

What you need
- cArt-us card: white 210 (P30)
- Bazzill card: pansy 640
- Harmonica template: no. 10 flower 2
- Ruler I
- Pattern C
- Marjoleine cutting sheet: purple Christmas
- Decorative border stickers: silver diamond

Blue candles

What you need
- cArt-us card: white 210 (P30) and cornflower blue 393 (P05)
- Harmonica template: no. 12 flower 4
- Ruler I
- Pattern E
- Marjoleine cutting sheet: blue candles
- Decorative paper: blue turquoise strips

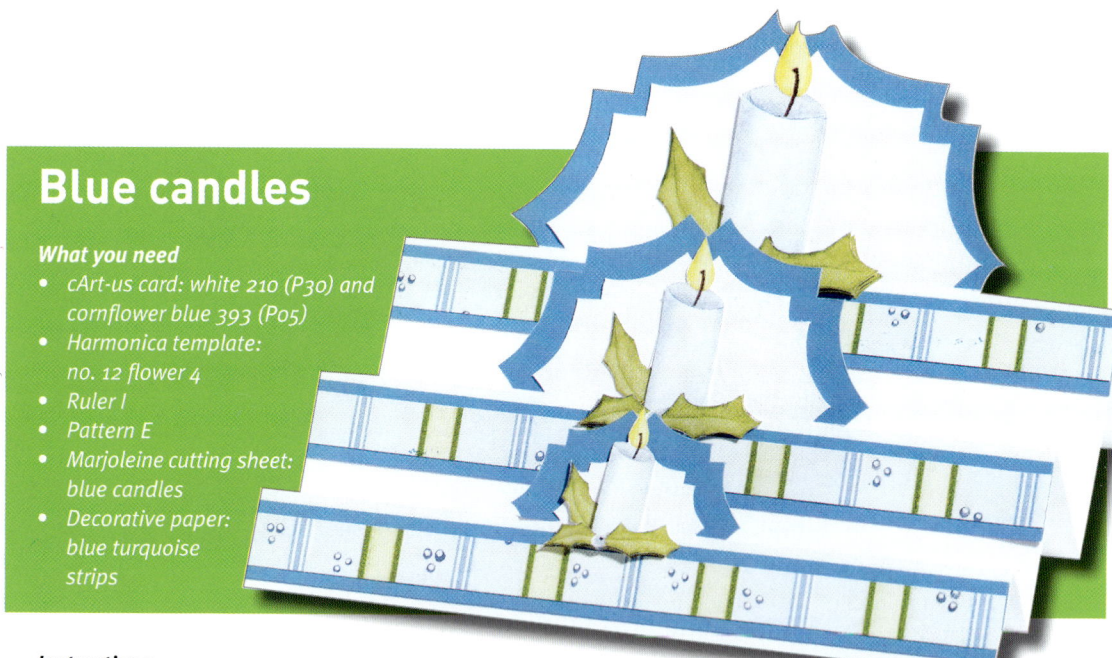

Instructions

1. Cut the card to size (14.85 x 21 cm). Cut, score and fold the harmonica card. Cut the smallest shape at the first > -sign, cut the 6 cm shape (indicated by arrows) at the second > -sign and cut the outer shape at the third > -sign.

2. Stick 1.5 cm wide cornflower blue strips on the card and decorate them with 1 cm wide strips of decorative paper.

3. Use pattern E to cut the half-shapes and stick them to the back of the card.

4. Stick candles on the card and make them 3D.

Pink candles

Instructions
1. Cut the card to size (14.85 x 21 cm). Cut, score and fold the harmonica card. Cut the smallest shape at the first > -sign, cut the 6 cm shape (indicated by arrows) at the second > -sign and cut the outer shape at the third > -sign.

2. Stick 1.5 cm wide mauve strips on the card and decorate them with 1 cm wide strips of decorative paper.

3. Use pattern D to cut the half-shapes and stick them to the back of the card.

4. Stick candles on the card and make them 3D.

What you need
- cArt-us card: white 210 (P30)
- Papicolor card: mauve P13
- Harmonica template: no. 5 labels
- Ruler I
- Pattern D
- Marjoleine cutting sheet: pink candles
- Decorative paper: green/pink stripes

Christmas

Christmas roses

What you need
- cArt-us card:
  cream 241 (P27) and old red 517 (P12)
- Mi-Teintes card: apple green 475 (P169)
- Harmonica template: no. 8 stars
- Ruler L
- Decorative sticker: yellow triangle lace border
- Marjoleine cutting sheet: Christmas roses

Instructions
1. Cut the card to size (14.8 x 29.7 cm). Cut, score and fold the harmonica card using the side with the single shape. Use the one from last outer cutting line.

2. Stick three apple green strips on the card (two of 1.5 x 14.8 cm and one of 2.5 x 14.8 cm). Use stickers to decorate the card.

3. Cut two half, old red stars and stick them on the card.

4. Stick a picture of Christmas roses on the card and make them 3D.

Christmas candles

What you need
- cArt-us card:
  cream 241 (P27) and old red 517 (P12)
- Mi-Teintes card: apple green 475 (P169)
- Harmonica template: no. 12 flower 4
- Ruler L
- Decorative sticker: yellow lace pattern
- Marjoleine cutting sheet: red candles

Instructions

1. Cut the card to size (14.8 x 29.7 cm). Cut, score and fold the harmonica card using the side with the single shape. Use the outer cutting line.

2. Stick three old red strips on the card (two of 1.5 x 14.8 cm and one of 2 x 14.8 cm). Use stickers to decorate the card.

3. Cut two half, apple green stars and stick them on the card. Use stickers to decorate the shapes.

4. Stick candles on the card and make them 3D.

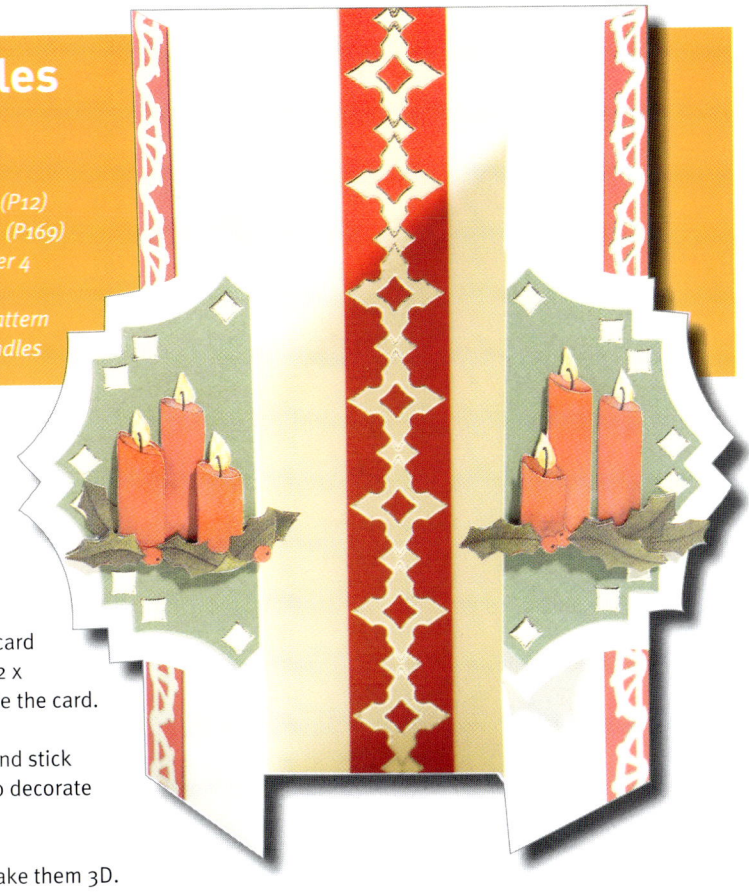

Three candles

What you need
- cArt-us card: natural 211 (P29), old red 517 (P12) and dark green 309 (P18)
- cArt-us paper: old red 517 (P12)
- Circle cutter
- Harmonica template: no. 10 flower 2
- MD cutting sheet: candles no. 3D464
- Pattern F
- Easy Punch corner punch: holly
- Sulky thread: gold 7007
- Decorative lace border sticker: transparent gold

Instructions
1. Cut a circle (Ø 14.85 cm) out of natural card. Place the template in the middle, cut the middle shape and score the straight lines using the template.

2. Copy pattern F onto old red paper and punch the semicircle. Cut through the narrow bridges between each punched shape. Use circle stickers to decorate the holes.

3. Cut a dark green semicircle (Ø 14 cm). Cut half a shape out of natural card and a whole shape out of old red card. Wind embroidery thread around the old red shape.

4. Stick everything on the card. Stick three candles on the card and make them 3D.

Pyramid candle

What you need
- cArt-us card: natural 211 (P29), old red 517 (P12) and dark green 309 (P18)
- cArt-us paper: old red 517 (P12)
- Circle cutter
- Harmonica template: no. 12 flower 4
- MD cutting sheet: candles no. 3D464
- Circle punch: elegant antique
- Making Memories stitches: primary colours
- Decorative lace border sticker: transparent gold

Instructions

1. Cut a circle (Ø 14.85 cm) out of dark green card. Place the template in the middle, cut the outer shape and score the straight lines using the template.

2. Use the circle punch to punch a large circle, cut it in two and decorate it with circle stickers.

3. Cut a natural semicircle (Ø 14 cm). Cut half a shape out of dark green card and a whole shape out of natural card. Wind embroidery thread around the natural shape.

4. Stick everything on the card. Stick a pyramid candle on the card and make it 3D.

Cards on page 1 and 3

Harry & Marja (page 1)

What you need
- cArt-us card: pink 481 (P34)
- Bazzill card: pomegranate 227 (P43)
- Harmonica templates: no. 6 flowers and no. 8 stars
- Ruler K
- Sirius frame sheet: white and pink flowers SHSV223
- Glass alphabet stickers: small letters
- Easy Punch: blue flower, yellow and green daisy and green circle
- Small pastel snaps and pastel eyelets
- Mini adhesive stones: pink

Instructions
1. Cut the card to size (7.5 x 15 cm). Cut, score and fold the harmonica card. Mark the middle of the first two lines and place one of the twin shapes level with this mark.

2. Cut a 6 cm flower shape for Marja and a 6 cm star shape for Harry out of card. Punch the flower shape for Marja and the daisies for Harry. Cut a pomegranate strip (1 x 7.5 cm) for Harry.

3. Put the pomegranate strip through the Xyron sticker maker and punch the circles.

4. Stick everything on the card. Add the eyelets and the snaps. Use adhesive stones to decorate the card.

Two candles (page 3)

What you need
- cArt-us card: natural 211 (P29) and dark red 519 (P43)
- Circle cutter
- Harmonica template: no. 11 flower 3
- MD cutting sheet: candles no. 3D464
- Scrap pad: tulip

Instructions
1. Cut a circle (Ø 14.85 cm) out of natural card. Place the template in the middle, cut the outer shape and score the straight lines using the template.

2. Cut a striped semicircle (Ø 14 cm). Cut a dark red shape and a natural shape.

3. Stick everything on the card. Stick two candles on the card and make them 3D.

Pattern B

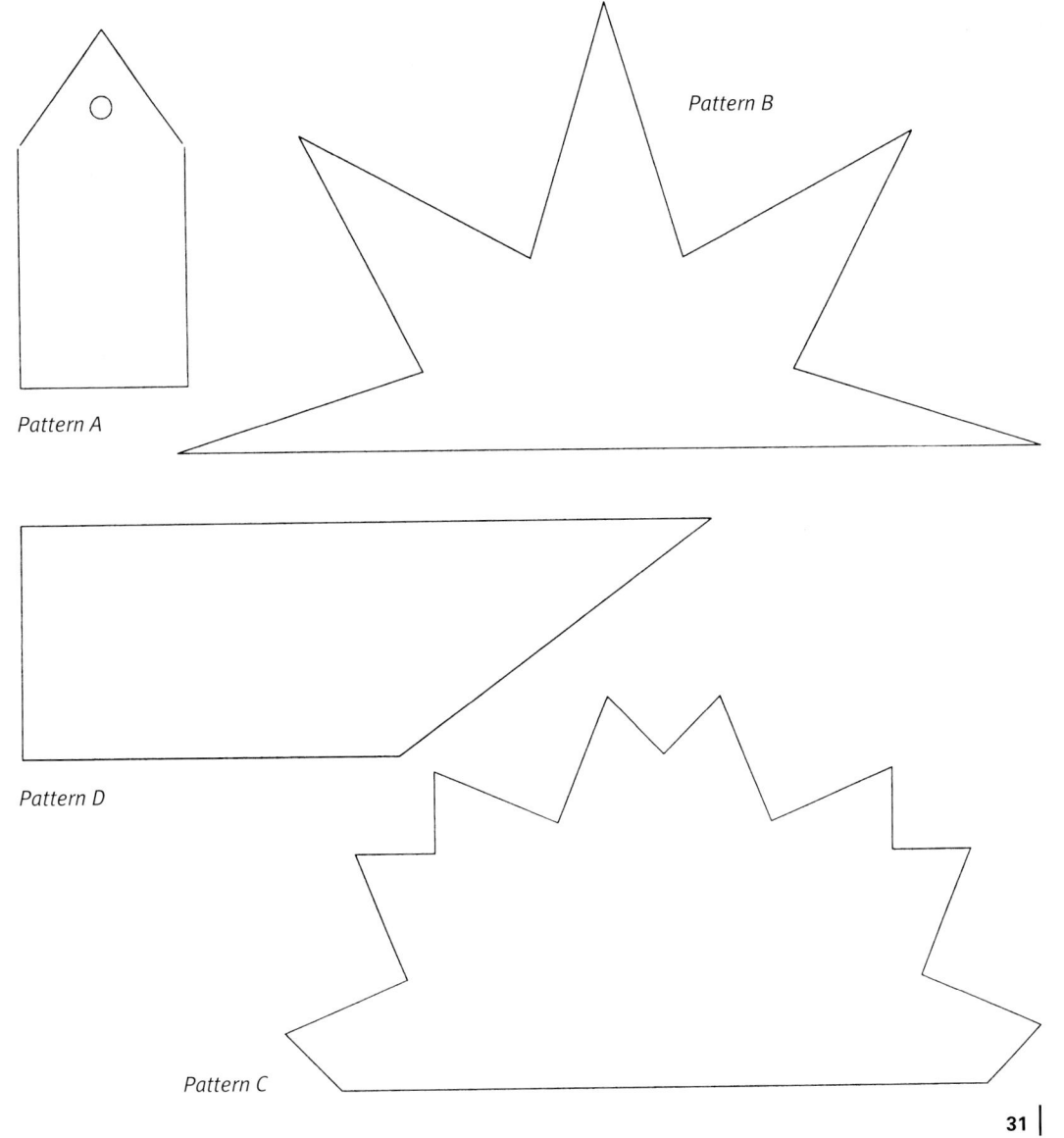

Pattern A

Pattern D

Pattern C

31

Pattern E

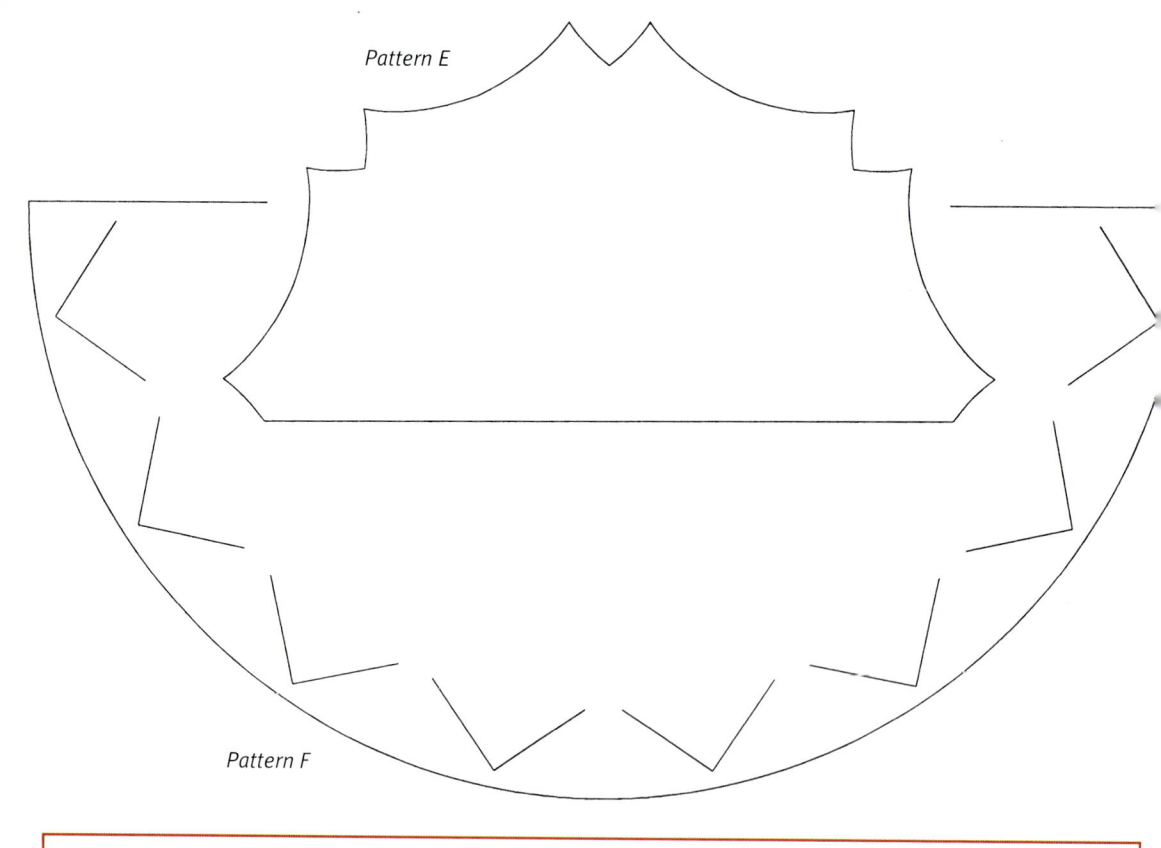

Pattern F

Many thanks to Kars & Co. B.V. in Ochten, the Netherlands, JEJE Produkt V.O.F. in Hilversum, the Netherlands, Sirius Hobby in Eindhoven, the Netherlands and Hobbyzaak Crealies in Amersfoort, the Netherlands, for providing the materials.

The materials can be ordered by card-makers from craft shop Crealies, Anna Boelensgaarde 23, 3824 BR Amersfoort, the Netherlands, +31 (0)33 4564052 (until 6 p.m.). The shop is open on appointment. E-mail: info@crealies.nl. Also see www.crealies.nl. If you wish to remain informed about what I have in store for you in the future, then complete the form on the website or send a card to the address given above.